9

VINTAGE

Murakami Diary 2009

VINTAGE

Published by Vintage 2008

2 4 6 8 10 9 7 5 3 1

All quotations and extracts from works by Haruki Murakami
© Haruki Murakami 2008
Layout and design © Vintage Design 2008

This book is sold subject to the condition that it shall not,
by way of trade or otherwise, be lent, resold, hired out,
or otherwise circulated without the publisher's prior
consent in any form of binding or cover other than that
in which it is published and without a similar condition,
including this condition, being imposed on the
subsequent purchaser

Vintage Books
Random House, 20 Vauxhall Bridge Road,
London SW1V 2SA

www.vintage-books.co.uk

Addresses for companies within The Random House Group Limited
can be found at: www.randomhouse.co.uk/offices.htm

The Random House Group Limited Reg. No. 954009

A CIP catalogue record for this book
is available from the British Library

ISBN 9780099523673

The Random House Group Limited makes every effort to ensure that the
papers used in its books are made from trees that have been legally sourced
from well-managed and credibly certified forests. Our paper procurement
policy can be found at: www.randomhouse.co.uk/paper.htm

Printed and bound in China by
C&C Offset

Again and again I called out for Midori from the
dead centre of this place that was no place.

Norwegian Wood

personal details

name

address

telephone **home**

       work

       mobile

fax

email

doctor

telephone

dentist

telephone

blood group

in case of emergency please contact:

name

address

telephone

name

address

telephone

New York   London   Tokyo

world time

calendar 2009

january

m	t	w	t	f	s	s
			1	2	3	4
5	6	7	8	9	10	11
12	13	14	15	16	17	18
19	20	21	22	23	24	25
26	27	28	29	30	31	

february

m	t	w	t	f	s	s
						1
2	3	4	5	6	7	8
9	10	11	12	13	14	15
16	17	18	19	20	21	22
23	24	25	26	27	28	

march

m	t	w	t	f	s	s
						1
2	3	4	5	6	7	8
9	10	11	12	13	14	15
16	17	18	19	20	21	22
23	24	25	26	27	28	29
30	31					

april

m	t	w	t	f	s	s
		1	2	3	4	5
6	7	8	9	10	11	12
13	14	15	16	17	18	19
20	21	22	23	24	25	26
27	28	29	30			

may

m	t	w	t	f	s	s
				1	2	3
4	5	6	7	8	9	10
11	12	13	14	15	16	17
18	19	20	21	22	23	24
25	26	27	28	29	30	31

june

m	t	w	t	f	s	s
1	2	3	4	5	6	7
8	9	10	11	12	13	14
15	16	17	18	19	20	21
22	23	24	25	26	27	28
29	30					

july

m	t	w	t	f	s	s
		1	2	3	4	5
6	7	8	9	10	11	12
13	14	15	16	17	18	19
20	21	22	23	24	25	26
27	28	29	30	31		

august

m	t	w	t	f	s	s
					1	2
3	4	5	6	7	8	9
10	11	12	13	14	15	16
17	18	19	20	21	22	23
24	25	26	27	28	29	30
31						

september

m	t	w	t	f	s	s
	1	2	3	4	5	6
7	8	9	10	11	12	13
14	15	16	17	18	19	20
21	22	23	24	25	26	27
28	29	30				

october

m	t	w	t	f	s	s
			1	2	3	4
5	6	7	8	9	10	11
12	13	14	15	16	17	18
19	20	21	22	23	24	25
26	27	28	29	30	31	

november

m	t	w	t	f	s	s
						1
2	3	4	5	6	7	8
9	10	11	12	13	14	15
16	17	18	19	20	21	22
23	24	25	26	27	28	29
30						

december

m	t	w	t	f	s	s
	1	2	3	4	5	6
7	8	9	10	11	12	13
14	15	16	17	18	19	20
21	22	23	24	25	26	27
28	29	30	31			

january

				1	2	3
4	5	6	7	8	9	10
11	12	13	14	15	16	17
18	19	20	21	22	23	24
25	26	27	28	29	30	

february

1	2	3	4	5	6	7
8	9	10	11	12	13	14
15	16	17	18	19	20	21
22	23	24	25	26	27	28

march

1	2	3	4	5	6	7
8	9	10	11	12	13	14
15	16	17	18	19	20	21
22	23	24	25	26	27	28
29	30	31				

april

			1	2	3	4
5	6	7	8	9	10	11
12	13	14	15	16	17	18
19	20	21	22	23	24	25
26	27	28	29	30		

may

					1	2
3	4	5	6	7	8	9
10	11	12	13	14	15	16
17	18	19	20	21	22	23
24	25	26	27	28	29	30
31						

june

		1	2	3	4	5
6	7	8	9	10	11	12
13	14	15	16	17	18	19
20	21	22	23	24	25	26
27	28	29	30			

july

			1	2	3	4
5	6	7	8	9	10	11
12	13	14	15	16	17	18
19	20	21	22	23	24	25
26	27	28	29	30	31	

august

						1
2	3	4	5	6	7	8
9	10	11	12	13	14	15
16	17	18	19	20	21	22
23	24	25	26	27	28	29
30	31					

september

		1	2	3	4	5
6	7	8	9	10	11	12
13	14	15	16	17	18	19
20	21	22	23	24	25	26
27	28	29	30			

october

				1	2	3
4	5	6	7	8	9	10
11	12	13	14	15	16	17
18	19	20	21	22	23	24
25	26	27	28	29	30	31

november

1	2	3	4	5	6	7
8	9	10	11	12	13	14
15	16	17	18	19	20	21
22	23	24	25	26	27	28
29	30					

december

		1	2	3	4	5
6	7	8	9	10	11	12
13	14	15	16	17	18	19
20	21	22	23	24	25	26
27	28	29	30	31		

Included in this diary is a selection of Japanese national holidays, seasonal days and festivals.

January 12 – 成人の日 (Seijin no hi) – Coming of Age Day. This national holiday is a celebration for young adults who turn twenty, the age of majority in Japan, between April 2 of the previous year and April 1 of the current year.

February 11 – 建国記念の日 (Kenkoku kinen no hi) National Foundation Day marks the date when, according to legend, Emperor Jimmu founded Japan in 660 BC.

March 3 – 雛祭り(Hina Matsuri) – Dolls' Festival. This celebrates Girls' Day, when families pray for their future happiness and prosperity.

March 5 – 啓蟄 (Keichitsu) – The Awakening of Hibernated Insects. A seasonal day celebrating the warmth of spring and the return of hibernating animals.

March 14 – White Day. Not a national holiday, White Day is believed to have been introduced to Japan by a marshmallow manufacturing company in the 1960s. The white marshmallows gave the day its name, but men also make presents of flowers, sweets and cookies.

May 4 – みどりの日 (Midori no hi) – Greenery Day.
Part of Golden Week, a collection of four national
holidays within seven days, Greenery Day is a day to
celebrate, and commune with, nature. Until 2006 it
was held on April 29 in honour of Emperor Hirohito
(d. 1989), who was born on this day in 1901.

May 5 – 子供の日 (Kodomo no hi) – Children's Day.
Also called Boys' Day, to distinguish it from March 3,
this national holiday brings Golden Week to an end.

July 20 – 海の日 (Umi no hi) – Ocean Day. Also known
as Marine day, this is Japan's newest national holiday,
first observed in 1996. It commemorates the safe
return of Emperor Meiji from a tour of Hokkaido
in 1876.

September 21 – 敬老の日 (Keiro no hi) – Respect the
Aged Day. Introduced in 1947, this holiday, which
celebrates the wisdom and achievements of the over-
seventies in a series of cultural and athletic events,
upholds a much older tradition of honouring the elderly.

November 15 – 七五三 (Shichi-go-san) – Seven-five-
three Festival for three- and seven-year-old girls and
three- and five-year-old boys. On this day, families pray
that their children will grow up happy and healthy.

November 23 – 勤労感謝の日 (Kinrō Kansha no hi)
Labour Thanksgiving Day is the modern version of the
rice harvest festival believed to have been held as long
ago as 678 A.D.

My birthday is January 4, 1951. The first week of the first month of the first year of the second half of the twentieth century. Something to commemorate, I suppose, which is why my parents named me Hajime – 'Beginning', in Japanese.

South of the Border, West of the Sun

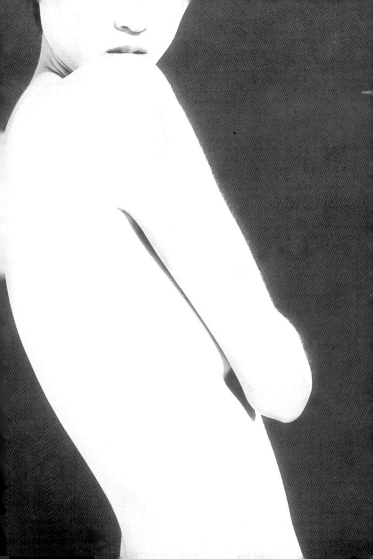

29

30

31

Something will work out tomorrow, I thought. And if not, then tomorrow I'll do some thinking. Ob-la-di, ob-la-da, life goes on. *The Elephant Vanishes: 'Family Affair'*

1 正月 (Shōgatsu) New Year's day
Holiday (UK and ROI)

2 Holiday (Scotland)

3

4

29	30	31	1	2	3	4	5	6	7	8	9	10	11	12	13	14	15	16	17	18
m	t	w	t	f	s	s	m	t	w	t	f	s	s	m	t	w	t	f	s	s
19	20	21	22	23	24	25	26	27	28	29	30	31								
m	t	w	t	f	s	s	m	t	w	t	f	s								

january 2009

5

6

7

8

9

10

11

12
1949: **Haruki Murakami** born

成人の日 (Seijin no hi) Coming of Age Day

13

14

15

16

17

18

The 1995 Great Hanshin Earthquake (magnitude 7.2 on the Ricter scale), usually referred to as the Kobe earthquake, was one of the most catastrophic earthquakes ever to hit Japan; more than 5,500 were killed and over 26,000 injured. It occurred at 5.46 a.m. (local time) on Tuesday, January 17, 1995 and lasted about 20 seconds. It was the largest earthquake to hit Japan in 47 years.

19

20

21

22

23

24

25 Burns Night

Strange and mysterious things, though, aren't they – earthquakes? We take it for granted that the earth beneath our feet is solid and stationary... But suddenly one day we see that it isn't true. *after the quake: 'Thailand'*

26 Australia Day

27

28

29

30

31

1 But in early February, again on a rainy night, she appeared.
South of the Border, West of the Sun

Through the driving snow,
I see a single white bird take flight.
The bird wings over the Wall and into
the flurried clouds of the southern sky. All that
is left to me is the sound of the snow underfoot.

Hard-Boiled Wonderland and the End of the World

2

3　立春 (Risshun) Beginning of Spring

4

5

6

7
Dance, Dance, Dance first published by VINTAGE 07.02.02
Title taken from rhythm & blues hit by The Dells

8
The Elephant Vanishes first published by VINTAGE 08.02.01
Underground first published by VINTAGE 08.02.01

I often dream about the Dolphin Hotel.
In these dreams, I'm there, implicated in some kind of
ongoing circumstance. All indications are that I *belong*
to this dream continuity.

Dance, Dance, Dance

9

10

11 建国記念の日 (Kenkoku kinen no hi) National Foundation Day

12

'I have to talk to you,' I said. 'I have a million things to talk to you about. All I want in this world is you. I want to see you and talk. I want the two of us to begin everything from the beginning.' *Norwegian Wood*

13

14 Valentine's Day
In Japan, women give chocolates to men

15

Then, all at once, I heard a sound. It came from somewhere far away – a funny, muffled sort of rubbing sort of sound. At first I thought it was coming from a place deep inside me, that I was hearing things – a warning from the dark cocoon my body was spinning within. I held my breath and listened. Yes. No doubt about it. Little by little, the sound was moving closer to me. What was it? I had no idea. But it made my flesh creep.

The ground near the base of the tree began to bulge upward as if some thick, heavy liquid were rising to the surface. Again I caught my breath. Then the ground broke open and the mounded earth crumbled away to reveal a set of sharp claws. My eyes locked onto them, and my hands turned into clenched fists. Something's going to happen, I said to myself. It's starting now. The claws scraped hard at the ground, and soon the break in the earth was an open hole, from which there crawled a little green monster…

The Elephant Vanishes: 'The Little Green Monster'

Haruki Murakami

THE ELEPHANT Vanishes

'A remarkable writer…he captures the common ache of
the contemporary heart and head' Jay McInerney

VINTAGE

16 I washed my face with great care, shaved, put some bread in the toaster, and boiled water for coffee. I fed the cat, changed its litter, put on a necktie, and tied my shoes. Then I took a bus to the elephant factory. *The Elephant Vanishes: 'The Dancing Dwa...*

17

18

19

20

21

22

23

24 Shrove Tuesday

25 Ash Wednesday

26 Greetings,
The winter cold diminishes with each passing day, and now the sunlight hints
at the subtle scent of springtime. I trust that you are well.

The Elephant Vanishes: 'A Window'

27

28

1 St David's Day

2

3　雛祭り (Hina Matsuri) Dolls' Festival

4

5　啓 蟄 (Keichitsu) Awakening of hibernated insects

After the Quake first published by VINTAGE 06.03.03

		2	3	4	5	6	7	8						
		m	t	w	t	f	s	s						

march 2009

White Day
The opposite of Valentine's Day: men give gifts to women

'There are only three ways to get along with a girl: One, shut up and listen to what she has to say; two, tell her you like what she's wearing; and three, treat her to really good food. Easy, huh? If you do all that and still don't get the results you want, better give up.' *Blind Willow, Sleeping Woman: 'Hanalei Bay'*

It's all too easy to say 'Aum was evil.' Nor does saying 'This had nothing to do with "evil" or "insanity"' prove anything either. Yet the spell cast by these phrases is almost impossible to break, the whole emotionally charged 'Us' versus 'Them' vocabulary has been done to death…

All I mean to say is that something in that encounter, in their presence, must also have been present in us to necessitate such active conscious rejection. Or rather, 'they' are the mirror of 'us'.

Now of course a mirror image is always darker and distorted. Convex and concave swap places, falsehood wins out over reality, light and shadow play tricks. But take away these dark flaws and the two images are uncannily similar; some details almost seem to conspire together. Which is why we avoid looking directly at the image, why, unconsciously or not, we keep eliminating these dark elements from the face we want to see. These subconscious shadows are an 'underground' that we carry around within us, and the bitter aftertaste that continues to plague us long after the Tokyo gas attack comes seeping out from below.

Underground

'Murakami shares with Alfred Hitchcock a
fascination for ordinary people being
suddenly plucked by extraordinary
circumstances from their daily lives'
Sunday Telegraph

Haruki **Murakami**
Underground

THE TOKYO GAS ATTACK AND THE JAPANESE PSYCHE

VINTAGE

16

monday

17 St Patrick's Day

tuesday

18

wednesday

19

thursday

20 春分の日 (Shunbun no hi) Vernal Equinox

1995: Tokyo Gas Attack leaves 12 dead and thousands injured. It was perpetrated by the doomsday cult Aum Shinrikyo

21

22 Mothering Sunday

23

24

25

26

27

28

29 Noboru Watanabe came riding up at three. Astride his trusty cycle, he arrived
with the gentle zephyrs of springtime. *The Elephant Vanishes: 'Family Affair'*

British Summer Time begins

Tohoku Color Agency/Getty

30

31

[The letter] was dated 31 March. After I read it, I stayed on the porch and let my eyes wander out to the garden, full now with the freshness of spring. An old cherry tree stood there, its blossoms nearing the height of their glory. *Norwegian Wood*

1 April Fool's Day

2

3

4

5

April was too lonely a month to spend all alone

In April, everyone around me looked happy. People would throw off their coats and enjoy each other's company in the sunshine – talking, playing catch, holding hands.
Norwegian Wood

Ole Christiansen/Getty

Wish I could talk to her. Half an hour would be plenty: just ask her about her-self, tell her about myself, and – what I'd really like to do – explain to her the complexities of fate that have led to our passing each other on a side street in Harajuku on a beautiful April morning in 1981.

The Elephant Vanishes: 'On Seeing the
100% Perfect Girl One Beautiful
April Morning'

13 Easter Monday
Holiday (UK, ROI, Aus, Can)

14

15

16

17

18

19

It was a clear Sunday evening near the end of April. The flower shops were full of crocuses and tulips. A gentle breeze blew, softly rustling the hems of young girls' skirts and wafting over the leisurely fragrance of young trees.
Sputnik Sweetheart

The sun rose the next morning and still Yamamoto had not returned. I was the last one to stand sentry. I borrowed Sergeant Hamano's rifle, sat on a somewhat higher sand dune, and watched the eastern sky. Dawn in Mongolia was an amazing thing. In one instant, the horizon became a faint line suspended in the darkness, and then the line was drawn upward, higher and higher. It was as if a giant hand had stretched down from the sky and slowly lifted the curtain of night from the face of the earth. It was a magnificent sight, far greater in scale, as I said earlier, than anything I, with my limited human faculties, could comprehend. As I sat and watched, the feeling overtook me that my very life was slowly dwindling into nothingness. There was no trace here of anything as insignificant as human undertakings. This same event has been occurring hundreds of millions – hundreds of billions – of times, from an age long before there had been anything resembling life on earth. Forgetting that I was there to stand guard, I watched the dawning of the day, entranced.

The Wind-up Bird Chronicle

Haruki Murakami

'Mesmerising, surreal, this really
is the work of a true original'
The Times

The Wind-up Bird
Chronicle

VINTAGE

20 *A Wild Sheep Chase* first published by VINTAGE 20.04.00

21

22 *The Wind-up Bird Chronicle* first published by VINTAGE 22.04.99

23 St George's Day

24

25 ANZAC Day
(Aus and NZ)

26 2009 Flora London Marathon
What I Talk About When I Talk About Running
to be published by VINTAGE in 2009

30 31 1 2 3 4 5 6 7 8 9 10 11 12 13 14 15 16 17 18 19
m t w t f s s m t w t f s s m t w t f s s
20 21 22 23 24 25 26 27 28 29 30
m t w t f s s m t w t f

april 2009

27

28

29

30

1 May Day

2

3

4 みどりの日 (Midori no hi) Greenery Day
May Day Holiday (UK, ROI, Aus)

5 立夏 (Rikka) Beginning of Summer
子供の日 (Kodomo no hi) Children's Day

6

7 From a nearby stand of trees comes the periodic scree-ee-eech of a bird, sharp as a tightening spring. The 'wind-up bird', we call it... This wind-up bird is there every morning in the trees of the neighbourhood to wind things up. Us, our quiet little world, everything. *The Elephant Vanishes: 'The Wind-up Bird and Tuesday's Women'*

8

9

10

27 28 29 30   1   2   3   4   5   6   7   8   9 10 11 12 13 14 15 16 17
m   t   w   t   f   s   s   m

18 19 20 21 22 23 24 25 26 27 28 29 30 31

may 2009

15

16

17 *Norwegian Wood* first published by VINTAGE 17.05.03

'How about your name?' I asked.
'May Kasahara. May... like the month of May.'
'Were you born in May?'
'Do you have to ask? Can you imagine the confusion
 if somebody born in June was named May?'
The Wind-up Bird Chronicle

The elephant's absence had first been noticed
at two o'clock on the afternoon of May 18...
The Elephant Vanishes: 'The Elephant Vanishes'

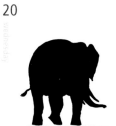

22

23

24

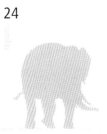

25 Spring Holiday (UK)

26

27

28

29 'I was born on May 29,' Creta Kano began her story, 'and on the night of my twentieth birthday I resolved to take my own life.' *The Wind-up Bird Chronicle*

30

31

1 *Birthday Stories* first published by VINTAGE 01.06.06
South of the Border, West of the Sun first published by VINTAGE
01.06.00

2

3

4

5 *After Dark* first published by VINTAGE 05.06.08

6

7

アフターダーク

Eyes mark the shape of the city.
Through the eyes of a high-flying night bird, we take in the scene from mid-air.
In our broad sweep, the city looks like a single gigantic creature – or more like
a single collective entity created by many intertwining organisms. Countless
arteries stretch to the ends of its elusive body, circulating a continuous supply
of fresh blood cells, sending out new data and collecting the old, sending out
new consumables and collecting the old, sending out new contradictions and
collecting the old. To the rhythm of its pulsing, all parts of the body flicker
and flare up and squirm. Midnight is approaching, and while the peak of the
activity has passed, the basal metabolism that maintains life continues
undiminished, producing the basso continuo of the city's moan, a monotonous
sound that neither rises nor falls but is pregnant with foreboding.

After Dark

アフターダーク

Joe Polillio/Getty

アフターダーク

A beautiful girl sleeping on and on in bed. Her straight black hair spreads over the pillow like a deeply meaningful fan. Softly pursed lips. Heart and mind at the bottom of the sea.

After Dark

8

9

10

11

12

13

14

15

16

17

18

19

20

21 夏至 (Geshi) Summer Solstice
Father's Day (UK, USA, Can)

'You got me,' she said, her back turned toward me as she shelled shrimps with her fingernails. 'There's lots we don't know about the wind. Same as there's lots we don't know about ancient history or cancer or the ocean floor or outer space or sex.' *The Elephant Vanishes: 'The Fall of the Roman Empire, The 1881 Indian Uprising, Hitler's Invasion of Poland, and The Realm of Raging Winds'*

22

The man before him was tall, thin, and wearing a black silk hat... He had on a form-fitting

23

as snow and fitted him perfectly. One hand was raised to his hat, as if he were tipping

24 Midsummer's Day

25

26

red coat with long tails, a black waistcoat and long black boots. His trousers were as light

27

politely to a lady... Looking at the hat, Nakata suddenly thought: *This must be the cat-catcher!*

28

Kafka on the Shore

29

30

1

Canada Day

It started on a perfectly beautiful Sunday afternoon in July – the very first
Sunday afternoon in July. Two or three chunks of cloud floated white and
tiny in a distant corner of the sky

Blind Willow, Sleeping Woman: 'A "Poor Aunt" Story'

2

3

4 Independence Day (USA)

5 *Blind Willow, Sleeping Woman* first published by VINTAGE 05.07.07

6

月
曜
日

7

火
曜
日

8

水
曜
日

9

木
曜
日

10

11

12

Noboru Wataya,
Where are you?
Did the wind-up bird
Forget to wind your spring?

The Wind-up Bird Chronicle

With the approach of autumn, a layer of long golden fur grows over their bodies. Golden in the purest sense of the world, with not the least intrusion of another hue. Theirs is a gold that comes into this world as gold and exists in this world as gold. Poised between all heaven and earth, they stand steeped in gold…But for the whites of their horns and the blue of their eyes, the beasts are gold. They shake their heads, as if trying on a new suit, thrusting horns into the high autumn sky. They wade into the streams; they stretch their necks to nibble on the autumnal bounty of red berries…

…When the horn sounds, the beasts look up, as if in answer to primordial memories. All thousand or more, all at once assume the same stance, lifting their heads in the direction of the call…

…For that one instant, all is still, save their golden hair which stirs in the evening breeze. What plays through their heads at this moment? At what do they gaze? Faces all at one angle, staring off into space, the beasts freeze in position. Ears trained to the ground, not twitching, until the dying echoes dissolve into twilight.

Hard-Boiled Wonderland and the End of the World

Haruki Murakami

'His fantasies, with their easy reference to western pulp fiction and music, retain a beauty of the mind' *Guardian*

Hard-boiled Wonderland and

the End of the World

VINTAGE

13

14 Thanks to his rare talent for keeping a diary over an extended period of time without missing a single day, he was able to cite the exact date his vomiting started and the exact date it stopped. It had started on June 4, 1979 (clear), and stopped on July 14, 1979 (cloudy).

Blind Willow, Sleeping Woman: 'Nausea 1979'

15

16

17
金曜日

18
土曜日

19
日曜日

20 海の日 (Umi no hi) Ocean Day
月曜日

21
火曜日

22
水曜日

23
木曜日

24 Let's see. July 24, 6.30 a.m. Ideal time of year for the beach, ideal time of
    day, the beach still unspoiled by people. Seabird tracks scattered about the
    surf's edge like pine needles after a brisk wind.
    A Wild Sheep Chase

25

26

27

28

29

30

31

金
曜
日

1

2

Every now and then, red birds with tufts on their heads would flit across our white and blue and yellow flowers and bees buzzed everywhere. Moving before my eyes. *Norwegian Wood*

th, brilliant against the blue sky. The fields around us were filled with
ead one step at a time, I thought of nothing but the scene passing

3

4

5

7 立秋 (Risshū) Beginning of Autumn

8

9

Spring passed, summer ended, and just now as the light takes on a
diaphanous glow and the first gusts of autumn ripple the waters of
the streams, changes become visible in the beasts.
Hard-boiled Wonderland and the End of the World

| | | | 3 | 4 | 5 | 6 | 7 | 8 | 9 | | | | | |
| | | | m | t | w | t | f | s | s | | | | | |

10 'Are you free today? I'd like to talk more.'

11

12 'Right,' she said. 'About my falling passionately in love with someone other than y

13

14

15 'You mean, about your falling in love with someone other than me?'

16

I clamped the phone between my head and shoulder and stretched. 'I'm free in the evening.' *Sputnik Sweetheart*

17

monday

18

tuesday

19

wednesday

20

thursday

21

22 Ramadan begins

23

All around me were the unmistakable signs of summer – the genuine article, without reservations or conditions. The glow of the sun, the smell of the breeze, the blue of the sky, the shape of the clouds, the whirring of the cicadas: everything announced the authentic arrival of summer.

The Wind-up Bird Chronicle

24

25

26

27

28

29

30

It finally hit me some dozen or so years later. I had gone to Santa Fe to interview a painter and was sitting in a local pizza parlour, drinking beer and eating pizza and watching a miraculously beautiful sunset. Everything was soaked in brilliant red – my hand, the plate, the table, the world – as if some special kind of fruit juice had splashed down on everything. In the midst of this overwhelming sunset, the image of Hatsumi flashed into my mind, and in that moment I understood what that tremor of the heart had been. It was a kind of childhood longing that had always remained – and would for ever remain – unfulfilled. I had forgotten the existence of such innocent, almost burnt-in longing: forgotten for years that such feelings had ever existed inside me... When the realisation struck me, it aroused such sorrow I almost burst into tears. She had been an absolutely special woman. Someone should have done something – anything – to save her.

Norwegian Wood

Haruki **Murakami**

'Murakami must already rank among the
world's greatest living novelists' *Guardian*

Norwegian
Wood

VINTAGE

1

3 That September afternoon toward summer's end, I took the day off and was lyi
in bed with her, stroking her hair and thinking about the whale's penis. The sea
a dark lead-grey. A brisk wind beating against the aquarium window. The lofty
ceiling, the empty exhibition room. The penis severed forever from the whale,
its meaning as a whale's penis irretrievably lost.

A Wild Sheep Chase

4

5

6

7 Labour Day (USA, Can)

8

9

10

11

12

13

31 1 2 3 4 5 6 7 8 9 10 11 12 13 14 15 16 17 18 19 20
m t w t f s s m t w t f s s m t w t f s s
21 22 23 24 25 26 27 28 29 30
m t w t f s s m t w

september 2009

14

15

16

17

18

19

20 Rosh Hashanah

Sunday morning I got up at nine, shaved, did my laundry and hung out the clothes on the roof. It was a beautiful day. The first smell of autumn was in the air. Red dragonflies flitted around the quadrangle, chased by neighbourhood kids swinging nets. *Norwegian Wood*

21 敬老の日 (Keiro no hi) Respect for the Aged Day

22 秋分の日 (Shūbun no hi) Autumnal Equinox

23

24

25

26

27

september 2009

Aura /Getty

28 Yom Kippur
Hard-Boiled Wonderland and the End of the World
first published by VINTAGE 28.09.01

29 Tuesday

30 Wednesday

1 Thursday

2

3 *Sputnik Sweetheart* first published by VINTAGE 03.10.02

4 1957: Sputnik I launched by Soviet Union

We were sitting as usual side by side at Inogashira Park, on her favourite bench. The pond spread out before us. A windless day. Leaves lay where they had fallen, pasted on the surface of the water. I could smell a bonfire somewhere far away. The air was filled with the scent of the end of autumn and far-off sounds were painfully clear. *Sputnik Sweetheart*

In the spring of her twenty-second year, Sumire fell in love for the first time in her life. An intense love, a veritable tornado sweeping across the plains – flattening everything in its path, tossing things up in the air, ripping them to shreds, crushing them to bits. The tornado's intensity dosen't abate for a second as it blasts across the ocean, laying waste to Angkor Wat, incinerating an Indian jungle, tigers and everything, transforming itself into a Persian desert sandstorm, burying an exotic fortress city under a sea of sand. In short, a love of truly monumental proportions.

Sputnik Sweetheart

Haruki Murakami

SPUTNIK
Sweetheart

'Murakami must already rank among the world's
greatest living novelists' *Guardian*

VINTAGE

monday

6

Kafka on the Shore first published by VINTAGE 06.10.05

tuesday

wednesday

thursday

9

10

11

28 29 30 1 2 3 4 **5** **6** **7** **8** **9** **10** **11** 12 13 14 15 16 17 18
m t w t f s s m t w t f s s m t w t f s s

19 20 21 22 23 24 25 26 27 28 29 30 31
m t w t f s s m t w t f s s

october 2009

12

13

14

15

16

17 Diwali

18 Then one Sunday afternoon in October, she rang up... A pleasant day, bright and clear, it found me idly gazing at the camphor tree outside and enjoying the new autumn apples. I must have eaten a good seven of them that day – it was either a pathological craving or some kind of premonition

The Elephant Vanishes: 'Barn Burning'

It was thirty-six past two by the clock when the telephone rang. Probably her – my girlfriend with the thing about blindfolds, that is – or so I thought. She'd planned on coming over on Sunday anyway, and she always makes a point of ringing up beforehand. It was her job to buy groceries for dinner. We'd decided on oyster hot pot for that evening.

Anyway, it was two-thirty-six in the afternoon when the telephone rang. I have the alarm clock sitting right next to the telephone. That way I always see the clock when I go for the telephone, so I recall that much perfectly.

Yet when I picked up the receiver, all I could hear was this fierce wind blowing.

Hokkaido's short autumn season was drawing to a close. The thick grey clouds in th

north were intimations of the snows to come. Flying from September Tokyo to

October Hokkaido, I'd lost my autumn. There'd been the beginning and the end, but none of the heart of autumn. *A Wild Sheep Chase*

23

24

25

British Summer Time ends

26

27

28

29

30

31 Hallowe'en

I can never forget how terrified I was that night, and whenever I remember it, this thought always springs to mind: that the most frightening thing in the world is our own self.

Blind Willow, Sleeping Woman: 'The Mirror'

1 All Saints' Day

2

3 1957: Sputnik II launched with dog, Laika, inside

The man-made satellite streaking soundlessly across the blackness of outer space.
The dark, lustrous eyes of the dog gazing out of the tiny window. In the infinite
loneliness of space, what could Laika possibly be looking at? *Sputnik Sweetheart*

4

5 Bonfire Night

6

7 立冬 (Rittō) Beginning of Winter

8 Remembrance Sunday

With marriage I took on not only a cohabitant bu

a new concept of cyclicity: the phases of the moon
The Wind-up Bird Chronicle

9

10 Once you start observing it closely, the human ear – its structure – is a pretty mysterious thing.
Blind Willow, Sleeping Woman: 'Blind Willow, Sleeping Woman'

11 Armistice Day

12

13

14

15 七五三 (Shichi go san) 'Seven-five-three' Festival

| | | | | | | | | | | | | | | | | 9 | 10 | 11 | 12 | 13 | 14 | 15 |
| | | | | | | | | | | | | | | | | m | t | w | t | f | s | s |

november 2009

monday

tuesday

wednesday

thursday

20

21

22

23

24

25 I still remember that eerie afternoon. The twenty-fifth of November. Gingko leaves brought down by heavy rains had turned the footpaths into dry riverbeds of gold. She and I were out for a walk, hands in our pockets. Not a sound to be heard except for the crunch of the leaves under our feet and the piercing cries of the birds.

A Wild Sheep Chase

26 Thanksgiving (USA)

27

28

29 Advent Sunday

All God's children can dance.

He trod the earth and whirled his arms, each graceful movement calling forth the next in smooth, unbroken links, his body tracing diagrammatic patterns and impromptu variations, with invisible rhythms behind and between rhythms. At each crucial point in his dance, he could survey the complex intertwining of these elements. Animals lurked in the forest like trompe l'oeil figures, some of them horrific beasts he had never seen before. He would eventually have to pass through the forest, but he felt no fear. Of course – the forest was inside him, he knew, and it made him who he was. The beasts were ones that he himself possessed.

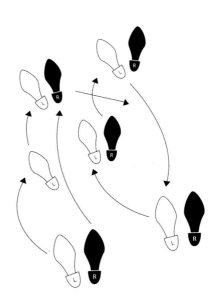

1 In 1987 *Norwegian Wood* was published in Japan. Murakami became a national celebrity. In December 1988 a Japanese weekly magazine announced 'HARUKI MURAKAMI HAS ESCAPED FROM JAPAN'

2

3

4

5

6

I imagine my search will continue – somewhere. A search for something that could very well be shaped like a door. Or maybe something closer to an umbrella, or a doughnut. Or an elephant. A search that, I hope, will take me where I'm likely to find it.

Blind Willow, Sleeping Woman: 'Where I'm Likely to Find it'

11

12 Hanukkah

13

From Sunday to Saturday, one Spaghetti Day followed another. And each new
Sunday started a brand new Spaghetti Week.

Blind Willow, Sleeping Woman: 'The Year of Spaghetti'

1971 was the Year of Spaghetti.

In 1971 I cooked spaghetti to live, and lived to cook spaghetti. Steam rising from the aluminium pot

tomato sauce bubbling up in the saucepan my one great hope in life...

Spring, summer and autumn I cooked away, as if cooking spaghetti were an act of revenge. Like

Blind Willow, Sleeping Woman: 'The Year of Spaghetti'

ide and joy,

rl throwing old love letters into the fireplace, I tossed one handful of spaghetti after another into the pot...

Spaghetti strands are a crafty bunch and I couldn't let them out of my sight. If I were to turn my back, they might well slip over the edge of the pot and vanish into the night.

14 R
   a
     i
       n
      d
        r
          o
            p
         s

15 beat against the glass, blurring street lights alongside the road that stretch
off into the distance at identical intervals as if they'd been set down to
measure the earth.

Kafka on the Shore

16

17

18

19

20

													14	**15**	**16**	**17**	**18**	**19**	**20**
													m	t	w	t	f	s	s

| 21 | 22 | 23 | 24 | 25 | 26 | 27 | 28 | 29 | 30 | 31 | | | | | | | | | | |

december 2009

21

22 冬至 (Tōji) Winter solstice

23

24 Christmas Eve

25 Christmas Day

26 Boxing Day

27

28

29

30

31 New Year's Eve

The most important thing is confidence. You have to believe you have the ability to tell the story, to strike the vein of water, to make the pieces of the puzzle fit together. Without that confidence, you can't go anywhere. It's like boxing. Once you climb into the ring, you can't back out. You have to fight until the match is over.

This is the way I write my novels, and I love to read novels that have been written this way. To me, spontaneity is everything.

I believe in the power of the story. I believe in the power of the story to arouse something in our spirits, in our minds – something that has been handed down to us from ancient times. John Irving once said that a good story is like a mainline*. If you can inject a good one into readers' veins, they'll get the habit and come back to you for the next one, no matter what the critics have to say. His metaphor may be shocking, but I think he's right.

Haruki Murakami, from the lecture 'The Sheep Man and the End of the World', delivered in English at Berkeley, California, USA, on November 17 1992.

*narcotic fix

Where am I?

Where do you think I am?

In our good old faithful telephone box.

This crummy little square telephone box plastered inside
with ads for phony loan companies and escort services.

A mouldy-coloured half-moon's hanging in the sky; the
floor's littered with cigarette butts. As far as the eye
can see, nothing to warm the cockles of the heart.

An interchangeable, totally semiotic telephone box.

So where is it? I'm not exactly sure...

Sputnik Sweetheart

David Muir/Getty

Malta Kano

Her name card was made of thin plastic, and it
seemed to carry a light fragrance of incense...
The card bore a single line of black letters...
Malta? I turned the card over. It was blank.
'Just my name. There is no need for me to
include my address or telephone number.
No one ever calls me. I am the one who makes
the calls.'
The Wind-up Bird Chronicle